A Butterfly's Transformation
In Poetry

A Butterfly's Transformation
In Poetry

by
Edmond E. Frank

Copyright 2021
by Edmond E. Frank

All rights reserved. No part of this book may be reproduced by any means or in any form without the express permission of the author.

ISBN 978-1-7348367-6-9

Sentient Life

It Is The highest form of life as we know it. Self-aware—Thinking—Feeling—Creating It's the kind of life that separates us from the lesser life forms.

We . . . are The Sentient Ones! And because of being so smart, we managed to tell ourselves a boat-load of lies to avoid taking responsibility for the truth.

Lies which we then pass on to our progeny, who like us, continue without thought to use those lies as rules to live by.

Sadly, as smart as we are, very few use that intelligence
to think for themselves—and to see the truth.

The other animals have no concept of responsibility. Life "just is," and is mostly a struggle to survive. We think ourselves above that struggle, and yet—those lies. . . .

We can twist the reality of our lives around to match ANY lie and make it the truth—in our minds. This book is dedicated to The Spiritual Laws. The REAL Laws of Life. Like gravity, these are the things that "just are"—and ALWAYS hold true.

It is the lies we have all been taught by mostly well-meaning people, and especially, the lies we tell ourselves that enable us to keep on trucking without any course correction—face it, it's those lies that run our lives into the fucking ditch. (Yes. This one deserves an F-bomb.)

I dedicate this book to
THE TRUTH.

Favorite Quotes

Love?
It's not how you feel about someone you've just met, someone with whom you are starting a relationship. The *truth* is about how you feel when it has ended. Doesn't matter what has happened in the meantime—all that doesn't mean *shit*. Fact is, if you don't love them and wish them the very best in the end, *then you never loved them at all.*

Redneck Spirituality—Book Two

Like the taking of offense, the ONLY functional use of judgments is when they concern your physical safety. Otherwise they are ONLY the shit between your own ears. Taking offense with people over your OWN judgmental mind insures your life will get stinky and very slimey. Unless it is a personal safety issue YOU do NOT have the right to control ANYONE besides yourself. Taking offense is ALWAYS about controlling others. Learn to control your judgmental mind. It is where your stinkiest shit is kept.

Redneck Spirituality Book Four

Table of Contents

NOTE:
There was NO poetry written for Chapters NINE or TEN.

Original Preface
2   *The Lesson*

Is War Ever Really About the Spoils—Ch 1
6   *What Would You Make of It?*
7   *What Then*

Who Mourns the Death of an Orphan?—Ch 2
12   *Sunny Hills*
14   *Alone*
15   *The Graveyard of the Orphans*

New Mommy—Ch 3
18   *New Mommy*
19   *What If*
20   *Of Shoelaces Trust and Self Esteem*

Fry Canyon—Ch 4
26   *Cowards*
28   *My Hero*
32   *I Am Who I Believe I Am*

The Bush Down Under—Ch 5
34   *My Trust ... In You, Dad*
35   *Death Adders ... Venom ... And Life*

Tarzan's First Puberty—Ch 6
40   *Balances*

Hanging With and Onto Mike—Ch 7
42   *Illogical Logic*
43   *Creating Joy in Life*

The Ozarks of Greece—Ch 8
46   *Heroes ... Cowards*

Reaching Through the Bars—Ch 9
❖ *This chapter had no poetry in the original manuscript*

Virginity: The Other Side of the Tracks—Ch 10
❖ *This chapter had no poetry in the original manuscript*

A One-Fingered Wave—Mike's Goodbye—Ch 11
52   *Mike ...*

Grantsville's Finest—Ch 12
54   *Red and Me*
57   *Mind Sight*

Graduation Night—Ch 13
60   *Mr. Dad*

Make Me a Man—A Stout Rodded Man—Ch 14
64   *A Hero in My Own Heart*

I, Predator—Ch 15
- 66   I Took
- 67   Obliviousness

The Land of Curly Nose Hairs—Ch 16
- 70   Like You
- 71   Something About Me

Meg's Story—Ch 17
- 74   A Mother's Love
- 75   Narrow Minds
- 76   Fatherly Love?

The Flashbulb of Fresh Love—Ch 18
- 80   All In The Bargain
- 81   Honey Bucket People
- 83   It's Me Here ... Now

Of Drippy Noses—Ch 19
- 86   Loving You ... Loving Me
- 87   Importance
- 88   Tears
- 89   Cheating

I Boom-Boom Only You—Ch 20
- 92   This Failure In Me

Hi-Ho Fuck the Army—Ch 21
- 96   Universal Consciousness
- 97   The Bottle
- 98   Shit Happens

Nah . . . Nah . . . Nah Nah . . . Nah—Ch 22
- 100 Destiny
- 102 Shit Rubs Off
- 103 Mr. Policeman, Sir

"F" Troop—Ch 23
- 106 Not About Right or Wrong
- 107 Quarrelsome People
- 109 Sgt. Ego . . . Sgt. Compassion

My Soul For a Dream—Ch 24
- 112 Double Standard
- 114 Who She Was

Back In the World—Ch 25
- 118 The Dragon of Fear
- 119 Surrogate Body
- 120 Help Me
- 121 Great Pain . . . Great Lesson

Victims Dramas and Control—Ch 26
- 124 The Blur of Love
- 125 Faulty Programs
- 126 Wand of Power
- 129 Marriage Vows of the Spiritual Warrior

A Goosed Gander—Ch 27
- 134 Saving
- 135 Hardships
- 136 No Coincidences

137 The Three Levels of Mind
138 The Real Danger
140 Expectations

Her Gift To Me—Ch 28
142 Of Attitude And Responsibility
144 Responsibility
145 Too Late
147 Love Never Hurts
149 Son
150 Life Ain't Always Fair

The Freedom of the Country—Ch 29
152 Life
154 Today
155 Sparring With The Dinosaur

Lessons of the Heart—Ch 30
160 Navajo Mary Begay
162 Lake Powell
163 Common Ground
165 The Crack In The Wall
166 Leaders . . . Traitors.
168 Run Away

Is This All There Is?—Ch 31
170 Of Eagles And Barnyard Chickens
171 "Goodbye Jeffrey"
172 Am I That Employee?
173 Perfect As God Made Them
174 I, Macho Man

Epilogue—The Ass End

- 176 Body And Spirit
- 179 Blame
- 181 As For Me
- 182 A Limp Dick No Longer
- 184 And That Hero . . . Is Me
- 185 Back In The Graveyard of the Orphans
- 187 Follow Your Heart
- 188 The Wonderment
- 189 Changing You
- 191 Mind Talk
- 192 Setting Up The Win

About the Author

Acknowledgments

The autobiographical novel *The Courage of a Butterfly* was a labor of love, on-and-off, for over 25 years. It could be said that it was the school ground for this writer's ability to write. And there have been numerous teachers scattered throughout the various critique groups over the years. It would be great if I could remember and acknowledge them all by name—but I can't. They are important to this book of poetry only in that these poems were written into the original manuscript to that novel. Nearly all those who critiqued it begged me to take the poems out. I eventually agreed .

I wish to thank *The Aliante Writers Meet-Up Critique Group*,
and the *The Sin City Writers Meet-Up Critique Group.*
Many in these two groups are published and all are excellent writers. They have been the most supportive to me. With the other critique groups, there was always the fact that many of the members were not of this venue—Self-Help, Spirituality, New Age, New Thought. But many of the Sin City group were. Those who weren't were mostly open-minded.

There were my beta readers:
Valerie J Runyan
Wanda Erekson
Dee Ann Leger
Tina Cummings
Susan Bradley
Nicola B Dipalma
Lillian Whelband
Jodeane Mccarty
Donna E Hollar

There is my editor and good friend Karen Diehl. The excellence of her work makes mine sound intelligent—sometimes.

There is Joylynn Ross of Pathtopublishing.com
Joylynn is another friend and mentor, an expert in the industry.

Lastly, there is Bobby of Bobby Daniels, Graphics my cover designer—probable the most important person in influencing you, the reader, to buy this book. He is a true artist and I highly recommend him to other writers.

Introduction—

Have you ever taken that "Road less traveled"—the one some call the "inner journey." Most folks are afraid to look within themselves—afraid of what they'll find. At the time I wrote these poems, my marriage was breaking up and so life was squeezing me. If you squeeze an orange, what comes out? Yeah well, I'm not an orange, it was poetry that was squirting out of me. At that time I was writing a memoir novel, *The Courage of a Butterfly*

These poems were originally distributed throughout that novel. They just naturally got immersed as part of the story. But for those who don't like poetry, they were just confusing bumps in the road of life—bumps that couldn't be skipped—and could send the reader into a skid.

So are these poems the REST of the story? Maybe they're the BEST of the story, or the DEPTHS of the story—NO. These poems are the HEART of the story. Yes, there were tears. But when one truly looks within and gets a glimpse of one's soul, there is also ecstasy. Why? For that answer, you'll need to read the mother novel that gave birth to these poems.

Yes, the story was written with tears—and also with joy. To go within and discover the truth of who you are, to see the wonder of it, is to be transformed. It is to experience MAGNIFICENCE—the wonder that every butterfly knows.

So what was the story line—and what was I, a redneck, doing writing poetry? Was I just staring into the headlights to even offer it up.

You might say it started with me in a hospital facing my imminent death. There is a presence that permeates an ICU. Some call it the presence of Death, some The Grim Reaper, and some just know it as The Angel (of Death).

In my own way, I met The Angel—knew him intimately. You see, you just can't tell that Angel the same lies you've been telling yourself throughout your life—the ones that allowed you to get out of bed every morning and go about your life without making drastic changes.

If you ever stopped telling them to yourself—and pretending to believe them—you would die. You see, when you change your mind, your beliefs about anything, your whole life changes. The old one stops—just dies—and a new one begins.

What holds us all from telling ourselves the truth is the price we'd have to pay to acknowledge it. With me, that price was my wife. I loved her so deeply and for so long, that I could not—no, make that *would not*—admit the truth. I was her security in life, but I was *never* the love of her life.

Thing was, for me to lie to The Angel at that point, I believe, would have definitely cost me my life—*my physical life.* I got honest and it did cost me my wife and everything else that then was of importance to me. The price was worth it. In the process I discovered the Spiritual Laws. They are merely those common-sense things that, like the Law of Gravity, always hold true.

As I see it, gravity is a physical law that was set down for this universe by its Creator. That Creator being the all powerful "omnipotent" essence of it all . . .

That says to me that the higher power most call God, actually IS the totality of it all. I am a part of this universe—I am as a drop in the vast Ocean of God, an actual part of God. Like DNA, I have it all—all the power I can possibly wield in the creation of my life.

And to that point, I had wielded it poorly. I did not like, respect, or even accept that person I was back then. As such I was pissing into the face of God.

Life—ALL OF IT—from what we eat to what we excrete; IT IS ALL GOD. Yeah, I know. Now I'm sounding like some religious zealot standing on a street corner raving.

Except, MY sign doesn't say—

      REPENT! THE WORLD IS AT AN END!"

No. My sign says—

> Open the eyes of your mind, see the truth—
> AND LIVE IT!

So, now, back to my statement—

> *Life—all of it—IS ALL GOOD. IT IS ALL GOD.*

You know how a fish doesn't know water until they're out of it—immersed in the air? Well despite what Organized Religions would have you believe, you don't need to go to church to find God. You are an actual part and piece of him/her. If you want to find God, look within yourself—but LOOK with the truth. That's a tall order, seeing how we have all been trained to lie to ourselves when life doesn't fit how we want it to be.

These laws—these truths—have been around every bit as long as the Bible. Most of it is just common sense. These truths are generally called Spiritual Laws—life is a spiritual event. The truths of life are therefore called Spiritual Laws.

Socrates was teaching them way back in ancient Greece.

> "The unexamined life is not worth living."

The truth is inside us all—built in. Except very few of us want to take responsibility of our poor choices in feelings whenever pissed off—much easier to blame someone or something else.

I discovered those laws, and with them I looked. Much of what came out of me was then poetry—THIS POETRY.

Me! This big tattooed, motorcycle riding, wrench turning, fucking redneck mechanic. Yeah, I EXCRETED it. It's ALL about life—about the TRUTH of it. And YEAH, for the third time . . . IT'S ALL GOD.

(I don't use the term "God" in a religious way. It is simply in a factual way of saying that Higher Power).

From The Original Preface

The Lesson

Mom . . . Dad . . .
You are as the dead to me.
Killed by your own vengeance.
Murdered by your rage. . .
I cannot contact you
without joining your war.
And that, I will not do.
But I can hold you inside . . .
There, speak with a higher voice of mind
to the sorrows between our hearts.
I can remember
all that we once were together . . .
and love you . . .
Love you through the bastions
of your animosity,
that only love can breach.
For I know that you really don't hate me.
It is just your perspective
of what I have done,
that you hate.

My divorce was a need . . .
a necessity to the well being of my soul.
But you cannot see my perspective,
as it would make yours wrong.
A weakness most of us have.
We must not be wrong.
Our world would crumble,
were our perspective of it, not so.
Understanding that . . .
Seeing it is only your fear filled weakness
driving you to war . . .
How can I but love you?
Oh, how I long for your loving embrace,
your heartfelt acceptance and welcome,
and the respect I once saw in your eyes.
But I cannot change your paradigm,
your perception of me.
And I cannot go home . . .
to be there for you in your old age.
Nor are you here with me in my loneliness,
to help heal this wound in my heart,
to soothe this ache in my soul.
I no longer have the haven of your home
nor the panacea of your love.

I must heal myself
and learn to accept the love of strangers.
Perhaps this is the lesson that the Universe . . .
that God . . .
has given me to learn.
And perhaps . . .
before you truly do die,
you may yet choose to love and accept me . . .
perhaps better than ever before.

Is War Ever Really About the Spoils?
Chapter 1

What Would You Make of It?

Most assuredly you know
the date of your birth.
Yet, except to celebrate
or resist one day per year,
does this affect your life . . .
right now?
But what if you knew
the date of your death—
Would it change your life today?
Would you live any better?
Would you have more joy?
Have the courage
to follow your heart?
And how would you think,
if you thought that day
might well have been
one in your past?
Would you feel like today
is a gift from God?
Would you make in it
something that lasts . . .
give memories of love
to all those you pass?

What Then

When I die . . .
when I'm dead . . .
what then?
Who will be there
to watch the ashes fall?
Into space . . . into eternity . . .
To mix and become one
with the good red soil,
in the cool shady canyons
beneath those magnificent
sheer sandstone cliffs . . .
Weathered whites, or golds, or reds
draped in shredded tapestries
of manganese black;
the ancient homeland
of the Anasazi.
Perhaps I was one . . .
in a former life.
I feel a kinship there . . .
a homecoming.
And what of this life?

Will there be a hole
in the fabric of humanity?
Will I be missed?
Whose lives have I touched?
Is this world a better place
because I drew breath?
Will some work of mine
survive the present?
Will there be multitudes
to shed bitter tears
and wail out
in their agony of loss?
Would that it were so . . .
But then,
that is just my vanity . . .
my ego speaking.
In truth, it will be a mere blink,
a single tick
of the clock of humanity,
and all remembrance
and trace of me will vanish.
Except for a fragment of bone,
lodged under a rock
in some dry watercourse . . .

Or a few molecules of magnesium
nurturing a cedar . . .
Or potassium in a flower . . .
Or perhaps, some calcium
in the tooth
of a playful little chipmunk.
I will become a part of, and one,
with the canyon lands.
It is enough . . .
And sometime, perhaps,
my soul will reincarnate.
And I will once again
walk these desert plateaus . . .
drink from the cool springs
deep in the shadowy canyons.
And perhaps I will sit
in the shade of a cedar,
admire the perfection
of a wild flower,
even laugh at the antics
of a joyful little chipmunk.
And perhaps . . .
I already have.

10—A Butterfly's Transformation IN POETRY

Who Mourns the Death of an Orphan?
Chapter 2

Sunnyhills

Named for sunlit rolling hills . . .
oak forests and grassy knolls . . .
A beautiful name . . .
beautiful setting . . .
for such an ugly orphan home.
A place to house the unwanted . . .
the unlucky . . .
the abandoned.
Little children . . .
Courageous, innocent souls . . .
Facing their fate . . .
being shaped by life.
And in the cold and dark of night . . .
wakes a child with cries of fear . . .
cries of loneliness . . .
abandoned to his nightmares.
Ah, but to wake the others . . .
That cannot be!
Quick, two straps tied over the bunk . . .
A sock to silence his fear. . .

*Then abandoned . . .
alone once more,
in silent strangled struggle . . .
Now fighting for life itself.
A tear streaked face . . .
a snot stuffed nose . . .
gasping . . . choking . . .
straining for air . . .
through the sweat-hardened,
gritty . . .
lessons, of his life.
Shaping him . . .
molding forever . . .
his lonesome soul.
Many were the nights,
many the years.
A child wakes to the dark . . .
to grit and strangling snot . . .
to the taste of dirty socks . . .
to Sunnyhills . . .
to fear.*

Alone

Alone again . . . in a crowd.
Left out . . .
How does this show up in my life?
Is this what I put out to the universe?
That I am an island unto myself . . .
Self-sufficient . . . needing no one.
An island?
Only in that I am alone.
Self-sufficient?
Sometimes I don't even remember,
or bother, to feed myself.
Need anyone?
I silently cry out my need . . . anguish in it.
Yet am unable . . . unwilling . . . to reach out.
All around, people are talking . . .
laughing . . . relating . . . enjoying one another.
Why am I most alone in a crowd?
I must have the courage to face my fear.
Become vulnerable . . .
I may not be accepted.
But then again . . .
I may.

The Graveyard of the Orphans

In the sweltering meadow
of grass and brambles,
edged by the cooling shading oak trees,
hallowed ground beneath a hill
crowned lonely by cross of white,
lies the graveyard of the orphans.

Crumbling stones turning back to sand
fan silent across the land,
marking sunken patches in the ground.
Growing weeds from the turning of the soil
over childhood dreams now turned to dust
in the graveyard of the orphans.

The disclaimed offal of the indiscreet . . .
abide in the shadow of generosity
where only strangers mistake as home.
Imprisoned again in eternal sleep
or freed forever into oblivion,
in the graveyard of the orphans.

Through eyes of four, yet aged evermore,
I looked and wondered that day . . .
Would ever these eyes of mine see five?
Or would I, too, be cold
beneath this sweltering place
beneath the graveyard of the orphans?

How many, I wondered, were the children here
had fought this fight in other nights?
Had they choked on snot and stinking socks,
before lying silent beneath these plots.
Perhaps the cross was for someone else's God
above the graveyard of the orphans.

How many have stood in my tracks that day,
and pondered these same thoughts?
If I do just right, everything they say . . .
Can I, too, escape this fate?
Or will my loveless life still end,
forever loveless in this place,
in the graveyard of the orphans.

New Mommy
Chapter 3

New Mommy

I have a new Mommy.
Joyously . . . jubilantly I pulled at your hand . . .
Dragging you . . . showing you around . . .
To all that I knew in that dispassionate place . . .
proclaiming my truth to the orphans there . . .
I sang it loud . . . in joyous triumph.
"I have a new mommy . . .
And she will love and care . . . for me!"
Unlike my brother, I accepted you . . .
welcomed you with open heart.
And unlike him, didn't consciously see . . .
that was only so . . . for me.
Yes, I accepted you in love . . .
You were ". . . my new mommy!"
Though you never accepted me . . .
I was never ". . . your new son."
Rather, only a substitute . . .
Like a rubber doll,
for that one you could never have.
For that one you would accept . . .
with love.

What If?

What if Mommy had wanted me?
What if there were love
in an orphan home?
What if adoptive parents
didn't expect perfection?
Would I still be me?
Would I be this me, I like . . .
right now
had those lessons not happened . . .
back then?

Of Shoelaces, Trust, and Self Esteem

I look down the blue of my corduroyed legs
to the free flung laces of my shoes.
It is because of me, that they swing so free . . .
Yes, they flap with delight, a comforting sight,
for I have a new mommy,
and she will tie them . . . just for me.

My heart is as light as my four year old feet,
skipping gaily into your room.
With joy and elation, I pull-off my ruse,
"Mommy, Mommy, come tie my shoes!"
Your anger and disgust wither my smile,
as into my face you unload,

"How many more times must I show you?"
Kneeling on the floor, just as before,
again you do the ritual.
"This over that, you loop this,
you loop that, over and under,
now you're done."

Then loosed with a flick, "Now YOU do it!"
Idly I toy with it, my heart not here,
on something I need not know,

You are my new mommy;
you will take care of me now . . .
I know.

Smiling shyly, I look up . . .
Look into your eyes,
your eyes of rage . . . bulging . . .
distended with the furor of your emotions.
I'm shocked at your unexpected fit,
and the spite in your eyes as the words hit.

"Whatever possessed me
to take on such a stupid little shit?
I should have had my head examined!"
From the closet, my suitcase,
thrown down before the dresser,
my single drawer jerked open.

All the possessions of mine,
All the worth of me.
"Get your things . . . get out!"
Through the blur of tears,
I pack my clothes.
Then out into the hall I shuffle.

The stuffed red horse,
My only friend . . . loyal companion,
tucked safely under my arm.
Together we feel the whoosh . . .
hear the slam of the door,
behind us . . .

The hallway dark . . . old and cold,
of an apartment house
built early in the century.
With the promise of the mines . . .
The boom of Bingham Canyon . . .
Like me; now, somehow sadly left behind.

Suitcase at the door, reaching . . . struggling,
both hands turning the brass knob.
Its touch is as frigid as this chill in my heart,
and the ice crystalled glass
in the long narrow pane . . . frozen too,
in the heart of the door's center part.

Outside the air is biting,
the sun, a dim disc in a coal smoke smudge,
breathed in a grunge on every frosted breath.

At the bottom porch step we stop.
Huddled together, my frayed friend and me,
I hug him tight to stop him of his shivering.

Staring down the narrow walkway
of snow banks cresting overhead . . .
Cold, oh so cold . . . the chill stabs at my nose
pulls tight the ice choked hairs inside.
How will we stay warm? Where will we go?
Is there a warm place somewhere to hide?

Eternity passes . . . then you come for us.
Taking us back inside,
to the warmth of your home . . .
and the coldness . . . of your ice sickle heart.
Tears you cry and say you love me . . .
Say you're sorry . . . Yet, I question every part.

Are the tears really for me?
Are you really sorry?
Can I ever believe your heart?
Are your words your decoy,
when you tell me
I'm a good little boy . . .

And though you say it,
how will it truly go?
You say you'll always take care of me.
Yet, I know . . . in my heart, I know . . .
that I'm not good enough . . . for you,
and you won't be there . . . for me.

Will it always be,
that the women I love will see . . .
what you now, have taught to me?
Will my love . . .
ever . . .
be good enough?

Fry Canyon
Chapter 4

Cowards

I am not a coward
if I don't label it so . . .
in my own mind.
Until then, it is only your belief . . .
your opinion of me . . .
and for me, simply untrue.
I am a coward only
when I believe me to be.

When I won't forgive myself my weakness . . .
deal with it in integrity . . .
When it is unacceptable . . . to me.
For the what I do, is not the who . . .
It is me who calls it weakness,
others might term it a strength.
People often discard as foolish,
what another claims is brave.

I must always be acceptable to me,
and step past, unscathed,
your judgmental beliefs.

And sometimes, to be acceptable to me,
I must do something I believe is stupid.
Fear challenges intelligence,
until one can see,
no man is ever totally fear-free . . .
everyone has his fears.

The brave are the ones
who face what they fear
and then take another step.
A hero is he, who does what he must,
despite the danger or the fear.
A fool is one, who does the danger,
simply to spite the fear.
A true coward is he who does nothing,
when he knows something must be done.

My Hero

Oh, Mike . . .
Long gone . . . so lost . . . much loved . . .
brother of mine.
Where would you be today
had you not so senselessly died,
in that blaze of gunfire,
doing your own rendition of "Desperado"?
Would you still be my hero?
Throughout our youth we had each other.
Except in the orphanage,
when we were torn apart,
a short eternity in time . . .
I was four and so alone.
For the first time in life,
there was no one
for me to call my own.
And then adoption . . .
given away, but together.
For me, I was just so happy
to have my big brother back.
No longer would I be alone.

Yet you were devastated . . .
Thrown away . . .
and by the one you loved the most.
Did you feel you were less?
Oh, so worthless . . .
And perhaps more than me,
knew yourself as not good enough.
Is that why you were so driven?
Constantly proving
your courage . . . your worth,
to the ghost of a mother . . .
who never was.
Why could you not see me?
How my own worth was lost,
on the cliffs of the Frying Pan.
Clinging over the abyss . . .
Unwilling, unable to follow.
Backing down inch by trembling inch.
I had not your age . . .
your grace . . . nor your strength.
For me . . . to go farther was to die.
Did you gain a measure of manhood

with taunts and boulders hurled from above?
Discounting your little brother . . .
worthless . . . much less than life?
Did you not see the price I paid;
the price for your moment of fun?
The stamp, "coward,"
worn on the inside of my forehead,
Impressed there by my hero,
accepted and owned by me,
for the next thirty-five years to be.
No matter how many cliffs I followed you up
or how many rivers I traversed behind,
hand over hand on a cable,
it stayed there . . . indelibly written . . .
clear as the day I wrote it.
Until came the day I thought my last,
and I could not . . . would not . . . die,
a coward in my own mind.
Death gave me another chance,
an opportunity to change.
To take a different path.
Marked by the signs:

Personal Growth . . . Self Respect . . .
Integrity.
And though the path is not easy,
as is true of life,
every gain must have its price.
I no longer have the wife I loved
or parents to cherish and respect.
You could say, I am alone again . . .
Yet, it would not be so . . . I have friends
who love, respect, and support me.
And once again,
there is a hero in my life.
A hero unseen, but simply there . . .
For that hero
Was always me.
It took some time
for me to see
Only I . . . Can save me.

I Am Who I Believe I Am

So many years . . . Oh, so many years . . .
Spent believing myself a coward.
And I am, exactly, who I believe I am.
Yet, I always had the potential
to be anyone I could want,
starting at anytime.
In any second of my life,
I can choose to change.
Why didn't I?
Was it easier to look outside myself
to find my hero in Mike?
To be forgiving . . .
Accepting of his faults
to love him unconditionally?
Why did I not see?
It would have been even easier . . .
more magnificent . . .
far more loving . . .
to find this also . . .
In me.

The Bush Down Under
Chapter 5

My Trust... In You, Dad

We visited cousins . . .
devious . . . irritating . . .
obnoxious younger boys,
forever teasing.
You forbid me Dad, to answer their taunts . . .
"If they throw the dirt clods,
don't you dare throw back!"
I failed you Dad . . .
I would not take the abuse.
'Twas just a small one . . . just once.
Yet you stormed in rage . . .
charged from the house . . .
Your fist was doubled . . .
a mighty swing . . .
a death dealing arc . . .
just once.
But for its breath in my ear
on its comet flight past . . .
with a grateful hiss, it missed.
It would have killed my body . . .
like it killed my trust . . .
in you.

Death Adders... Venom... And Life

A snake . . . sunning on a porch.
At peace with its world.
Seeks only to live . . .
living to be free.

Yet I, upon seeing it,
pursue only its death.
While it slithers off, avoiding . . .
seeking only to be free.

Why would I want it dead?
It's not evil . . .
does not hate me.
It seeks only to be free.

Is it in my fear that I attack?
It holds the death . . . the ability . . .
the potential to kill.
Yet, it seeks only to be free.

Why not give it the same respect . . .
the same space it gives to me.
Why would I kill it . . . or it kill me.
We both . . . just seek to be free.

Why war with absurd possibilities?
With no Death Adders in the bush . . .
will the bush be where one wants to be?
Will Mankind then feel free?

When I kill off all danger,
take the spice from my life . . .
What then . . . is the point,
If freedom is a lack-luster right?

Was a snake between mother and me?
Did I face a venomous bite
when facing the venom
in her perceived sad life?

Did she sacrifice her life
to be a Mother to me
rather than let others think
what they were pleased to think?

Would her life have been better
had I just given up my fight . . .
Had I strangled on the realities
in the dark of my night?

No! Could never be so.
I am the danger . . . no mystery.
For the spice in her life is blame . . .
blaming me for her misery.

It sets her free of all she could be . . .
living in self responsibility.
Some only think they want to be free,
when in fact, we are . . . indubitably.

It is my choice.
I am free to believe
or free not to believe.
My Thoughts are created only by me.

Creation comes with each choice.
Conscious or not, they are what we want.
Everything exactly how it needs to be.
For us to become more than we were being.

Blame, too, is free . . . the venom in our bite
When with Death Adders or sacrifice . . .
we blame and we fight,
 It is only our love that we kill,
the love that gives light to our night

Tarzan's First Puberty
Chapter 6

Balances

Balances . . .
The Universe always balances . . .
What I give . . .
I get.
For every loss . . .
a gain.
Every gain . . .
a price.
If my experience
brings pain . . .
I need but look
to the joy behind
For the Universe is always
in balance.

Hanging With and Onto Mike
Chapter 7

Illogical Logic

Are my charms more attractive . . .
when I'm pointing out your zits?
Does my light make yours dimmer . . .
When I'm standing in front of it?
Do I appear any quicker . . .
by laughing at your wit?
Does one show his bravery . . .
by displaying his brother's fears?
No . . . Those things only show
the smallness of one's mind . . .
and the darkness
choking the light from his soul.

Creating Joy in Life

Life is perception . . .
and perception
a choice.
To you Mike . . .
Was your joy in the climb,
pitting your strength
against the cliff,
trusting yourself . . .
that you would not fall or quit?

Trusting to the death
for the joys you find
in conquering of the heights.
For me the heights are dizzying;
an unpleasant fright.
Not worth the price
to challenge the cliff . . .
no joy found
in pitting myself against it.

For me . . .
the joy is in the ride.
The wind in my face . . .
the road rushing by.

Yet, is it the same for me now
as was for you then?
Do I, too, not pit my strength and skill
for the return of the thrill?

The banking force of the turn . . .
the grip of the tires . . .
my butt in the saddle . . .
my soul a-fire.

All despite the whiz of traffic
inches by.
One slip from me,
as was true for you,
means death.

An everyday chance I take,
one that requires my best.
But was it the same?
No, mine was not the same strife.

You yearned for oblivion.
I for the joy in my life.
I face death to live.
You faced it to die?
A coward is he who closes his eyes;
not seeing life, or death, pass him by

The Ozarks of Greece
Chapter 8
Chapters 9 & 10 had no poetry in the original manuscript

Heroes... Cowards

I saw you as brave . . .
courageous . . . unafraid.
Strutting through life . . .
No matter the risk . . .
No matter the danger.
You took every dare . . .

But were you?
Death held little fear for you . . .
as it did me.
Life . . .
Was it of life
that you were afraid?

Afraid to live
as living held pain . . .
of being unacceptable . . .
unlovable?
From that you cowered
in abject terror?

Yet, I faced my cowardice . . .
my fear of heights . . .
of danger . . .
of death.
In support of you,
I walked on through.

And from this side I see . . .
how you succumbed . . . resigned;
died in a blaze of gunfire.
Were you a hero facing death?
Or a coward
not facing life?

It does not matter, my perspective of you.
Only the one through which I view me.
Thank you, Mike, my brother . . .
for teaching me to see
the courage that is in me.
Always there, but never before seen.

Reaching Through the Bars
Chapter 9
This chapter had no poetry in the original manuscript

* * *

Virginity: The Other Side of the Tracks
Chapter 10
This chapter had no poetry in the original manuscript

A One-Fingered Wave—Mike's Goodbye
Chapter 11

Mike...

Your death held no surprise . . .
little initial grief . . . only relief.
Relief that I played no hand.
Held no fault . . .
no responsibility.
I did not let you down . . .
It was not because of me that you died.
I believed myself the weaker.
Yet, always upheld you . . . supported you.
Cut you down from your suicide . . .
breathed life back into you . . .
saved you from yourself.
In the end, I was not there,
when you foolishly . . . uselessly . . .
faced down the Law.
Did you really think your twenty-two,
could match his thirty-eight?
Was it your bravado . . . your bluff . . .
Or did you just not care
to live . . . or to die . . .
to love . . . or to kill.
Oh Mike, my brother,
my hero . . .
I knew you not.

Grantsville's Finest
Chapter 12

Red And Me

Into the summer's heat, just Red and me.
Headed out across the wide desert stretches.
Vast panoramas between towering naked peaks
of desert ranges.
Open vistas, hung with early morning haze.
Promising a hot day . . . and freedom.
Just Red and me . . . headed out.
Our old Chevy of vintage forty-nine,
loaded down with supplies of food,
water, gear, and even our hard-won stash
of smokes and beer.
Headed for a week's freedom . . .
Days of hunting rabbits,
shooting our guns in the bright daylight.
Sitting around a cedar fire
smoking . . . shooting the shit . . .
and drinking beer by night.
Dugway Pass . . .
And geodes dug from Dugway clay.
Hollow spheres of crystal lined wonder.
Cracked open to disappointment . . .
Or sometimes, awed surprise . . .
Man's first view of nature's finery sparkling inside

Witnessed inside our tent,
by the glow of flashlight.
An afternoon's hunt with twenty-twos
yields an evening's dinner . . .
rabbit roasted on a stick.
And us, the proud hunters,
savoring it.
Then on to Topaz . . .
The mid-morning sun
upon the mountain
Heat waves dancing . . .
Sweating . . . sweltering in the glare.
Into the mountain itself,
a huge amphitheater
of grey rhyolite and white sands,
a-sparkle with the flashes . . .
tiny topaz crystals everywhere.
First we lunch . . .
from cans of beans and beer.
And then we sift the sands.
Our reward,
a handful of topaz sparkling clear,
and one lone garnet.
With crack hammers and chisels,
we climb the craggy heights,

*Hammers ringing . . . prying . . . splitting . . .
with passion we attack.
Opening cracks and crevices,
to an occasional hollow vug. . .
The thrilling pleasure
when filled with the sparkle,
the yellow-pink sherry . . .
of topaz.
And whooping with glee,
we unearth our treasures,
just Red and me . . .
All too soon . . .
our time is through.
And tired and happy,
we head back in . . .
Proudly sporting a week's growth . . .
a couple dozen scraggly hairs
on our smiling,
begrimed chins.
Back to the daily grind,
our summer vacation
of changing tires
and pumping gas.
To await again,
our pleasure ration.*

Mind Sight

When I don't open my mind to look,
I only see what I want to see.
If I don't see you . . .
who you are . . .
who you want to be . . .
you'll only be,
who I want you to be,
to me.

Graduation Night
Chapter 13

Mr. Dad

Yes, Mr. Dad . . .
Tonight's the night . . .
a landmark in my life.
One not happening . . .
the way I would like.
Oh, but to experience . . .
The nectar . . .
of a fruit so ripe.
Yes, I'm young . . .
My hormones moan . . .
and groan . . .
even howl . . .
a serenade to your daughter.
Her small firm breasts . . .
pert nipples . . .
lithe body
raise the want . . .
the expectations.
A desire for a meeting
within her . . . by me.
I know you, Mr. Dad . . .
'cause you remember me.
I am your worst nightmare . . .

and your fondest dream.
I am your most memorable memory.
So you take up my time,
keeping me in this space,
discussing your stupid . . .
fucking . . . fireplace.

Make Me A Man—A Stout Rodded Man
Chapter 14

A Hero In My Own Heart

Our founding fathers
all . . . had a choice . . .
an awesome opportunity . . .
to stand for what they believed in.
To put their fortunes . . .
their health . . .
their honor . . .
their very lives on the line . . .
by signing the constitution.
I, too, had that choice . . .
that distinction . . .
that awesome opportunity . . .
to stand for what I believed in.
To state it at the risk of my all . . .
to rise above my mortality . . .
to become a hero in my own heart.
In answering my country's call,
I stood forth in vulnerability . . .
and honor . . .
within.

I, Predator
Chapter 15

I Took

Two young women . . .
beautiful . . . sensuous.
One willing of sharing . . .
enjoying of her charms,
together with me in beauty.
The other saving . . . holding hers . . .
a present . . . a gift . . .
for someone special.
With both, I accepted the challenge . . .
With both . . . won the prize.
Yet in the winning,
from one I took . . .
the other I gave . . .
Then in the end,
from her also . . . I took.
With deceit, I took.
The real loss was from within.
I took beauty from my insight,
whenever my soul . . .
looked upon me,
with its light.

Obliviousness

I never lived in malice . . .
intentionally harming . . .
causing pain.
Physical pain . . . mental pain . . .
spiritual pain,
such was never my intent.
Rather, I lived my life in unawareness.
Covering my wants . . . my needs . . .
my own pleasures . . .
unmindful of yours.
Making myself right . . .
you, usually wrong.
Only wanting to win . . .
never seeing you lose.
Blind to the possibilities,
for you to win too . . .
That living my life in win-win,
is living my life in love.

The Land of Curly Nose Hairs
Chapter 16

Like You

I am a big man . . .
tall . . . muscular . . .
People remark saying,
"I see the strength in you."

In me? . . .
I suspect they only see me physically,
because inside . . .
I don't feel so strong.

I think inside I am the same as you.
I have my fears . . .
my insecurities . . . weaknesses . . .
though I don't let them show.

For they would say I need love . . .
like you.
And more . . .
I need to give love too.

And ultimately more so . . .
I need to be accepted
by you . . .
No . . . I don't see the strength in me.

Something About Me

What you see in me . . .
about me . . . concerning me . . .
are the judgments of your mind,
as seen through the colored glasses
of your life.
If you see it about me,
it is really, always, about you.
Yet still, I will take note . . .
examine what you say.
For I want my mind open,
to what I don't see, about me.
Yet, when the same
shows more in other ways . . .
through other people . . .
When life repeats the same message.
Then it is, I know . . .
there is always something,
for me to see . . .
about me.

Meg's Story
Chapter 17

A Mother's Love

A mother . . .
protecting her child . . .
the life of her child . . .
is necessary.
Yet only expected of a mother
or of any human adult.

A mother giving up her child . . .
protecting her child from hardship,
is foolish.
The human spirit . . .
child's or adult's,
can overcome mere hardships.

Deprivations . . .
not having enough . . .
enough food . . . good clothes . . . social status.
Yet, lack of love, a mother's love . . .
the nourishment of the soul . . .
is death to a spirit without.

Mother . . .
If you will not love your child,
or cannot protect
its very life . . .
Then . . . only then . . .
give it away.

Narrow Minds

If I close my eyes,
I need not see your suffering,
nor offer my help.
If I close my ears,
I need not hear your viewpoint,
when it doesn't fit mine.
If I close my heart,
I need not risk rejection of my love,
nor give acceptance to yours.
Yet if I do this,
I will need close my mind.
For if not,
I may see just what I miss,
and know that living my life this way,
is asking my soul for death . . .
MY death.

Fatherly Love?

A father, lovingly sheltering his daughter
from the harsh realities . . .
the evils of this world . . .
the cruelties of man.
Never prepared her . . .
Never protected her . . .

Naively taken . . .
Cruelly used . . . abused.
How could she set her boundaries,
without the knowledge?
The protective knowledge . . .
never taught.

A woman's most precious gift to a man . . .
To be lovingly . . .
freely, shared in beauty,
is turned to ugliness . . . loathsomeness,
when taken brutally . . . unwillingly,
by cruel men of despicable spirit.

A sweet young innocent,
ruthlessly abused,
through no fault . . .
no intent of her own.
Now dirtied . . .
The unacceptable shame
of a once loving father.

Rejected . . .
No longer fit to call her his own.
The daughter of a father,
A father unwilling to accept his fault . . .
his failure to prepare . . .
to protect.

Or to lovingly comfort . . .
to nourish her broken spirit.
A father not there
when desperately needed.
Oh, the price of his pride . . .
the shame of his ego.

The Flashbulb of Fresh Love
Chapter 18

All In The Bargain

Every bargain . . .
every agreement . . .
needs to be a win for both.
For the Universe always balances,
and in the end,
both parties will pay an equal price.

Yes, in the final shake down,
the Universe always balances.
I made a bargain
for a woman's company.
Yet disregarded her distress . . .
her feelings . . . the fairness to her.

I only saw the win for me . . .
never caring, not seeing . . .
the loss for her . . .
I bought her company . . .
But not the company I wanted . . .
only the company I paid for.

Honey Bucket People

There are those I pass on my path in life
who carry with them an air . . . an energy;
putrid . . . foul . . . disgusting . . .
an energy they have picked up . . .
collected along their path.
A path through the seamier side of life,
and an energy they choose to hold.

I cannot change them . . .
move them from their chosen path,
except by example,
a representation of a place
they would rather want to be.
Yet it is a place they must see . . .
must want to see.

Walking the alleys yoked . . .
a bucket swinging on each side . . .
Empting the privies of the privileged
It is not the yoke on their shoulders,
holding them apart,
but the shit between . . .
that shit between their ears.

Asking them to look will get me spilled on . . .
Slimed by energies I do not want.
Far better to travel my own path.
Climbing the mountain of life . . .
extend my hand of help,
only to those reaching
and leaving their honey buckets behind.

It's Me Here... Now

Am I the first love . . .
best love?
What does it matter?
Why should this affect my life,
as it is, right now?
Jealousy is the product
of an ego's poor self esteem.
Better to shout out my joy . . .
My exaltation . . .
Shout it from the highest peak.
Of all the men in the world,
who she could pick,
she chose me . . .
I am her man!
Here . . . Now . . .
Oh, how well I will love her . . .
Here . . . Now . . .
Forever.

Of Drippy Noses
Chapter 19

Loving You... Loving Me

As I loved this woman,
I felt only my own love,
my emotions . . . not hers.
Yet when she loved me back . . .
when she felt her own love for me,
I knew it . . .
and was uplifted . . . encouraged.
The energy of my spirit
soared with hers . . .
reaching heights unimaginable . . .
unattainable . . .
alone.

Importance

Your dreams . . . your goals . . .
the things of your heart . . .
are as much my concern
as you are.
If they hold meaning for you . . .
they must also for me . . .
if you do.

What is of importance in your life
must be also in mine . . .
equally as important . . . as you.
Those beliefs you hold dear in your mind
I must understand in mine . . .
if I want to know you . . .
if I truly love you.

Tears

A woman's tears . . .
are for feeling . . .
loving . . . nurturing . . . healing,
and most of all . . . are accepted.
And yet . . . for a man,
tears only mean weakness . . .
shame . . . embarrassment.
Why can a man not cry?

For with a man, it is accepted . . .
sometimes encouraged . . .
to express his pain through rage.
Slamming this . . . tearing that . . .
breaking things.
That, to some, is manly.
In reality, rage is only a poor substitute
for tears . . . healing tears.

Cheating

She was my woman . . .
most precious love . . .
cheating on her word . . . on herself.
Fulfilling obligations to those she loved . . .
helping her family . . .
at the expense of her honor . . . her soul.
Getting them the money . . .
exchanging it for the only value she knew:
her body . . . and her self-respect.
Oh, so cheaply sold.
But that is of her . . .
what of you, Lieutenant?
What were you buying?
Was it only a moment
of making your cock feel good?
No attachments . . . no responsibilities . . .
Or was it a moment
of making your ego feel good?
Tasting what was not yours . . .
of being better than me?

Paying with more than money . . .
paying with your integrity.
And what of me?
I got a drippy nose because of it
and a valuable lesson on caring.
But oh, the pain . . .
the necessary pain.
It took the pain,
for me, to find the gain.

I Boom-Boom Only You
Chapter 20

This Failure In Me

Unconditional love . . .
is to love without expectations . . .
restrictions . . . or limits.
It is to love you for who you are,
not for what you do . . . or don't do.
It is to accept you . . . without change . . .
without need of betterment.
It is to forgive you the mistakes I perceive.
For they are only my perceptions,
my judgments, making you wrong.
In unconditional love, you are never wrong . . .
There is no right or wrong . . . there just is.
You cheated . . . had sex with another.
To forgive, loving you unconditionally,
I have to accept your act . . .
just something you did . . .
not who you are.
For I know your heart is beautiful.
The pain I feel, is created in my own mind.
It is me who hurts me . . . not you.
Should you repeat your act . . .
repeatedly . . .
and I repeatedly choose the pain,

then, perhaps is the time
to accept the failure in me . . .
my failure to love you . . .
accept you . . . unconditionally.
And perhaps, then is the time
to change my life . . .
search out another . . . I will.
One who won't do the things you do.
So I need not struggle
with this weakness in me.
This failure I won't overcome.
This failure in me . . .
I won't accept about you

Hi-Ho Fuck the Army
Chapter 21

Universal Consciousness

My conscious mind . . . it's ego . . .
and the personality I know . . .
is only a small part . . .
like the tip of the iceberg . . .
or the mound of the volcano . . .
of my soul.
For my higher mind;
that part of me,
my consciousness only senses
but to which it wants to ascend.
From the bottom most frozen tip of ice . . .
to that high peak spewing fire,
when in true touch within . . .
is a part of me . . .so much higher.
My soul . . . touching all . . .
all of mankind . . .
the universal consciousness . . .
a part of and one with God.
The evil I do to one, I do to all . . .
to myself . . . even to god.
Yet, the love I give to one . . .

The Bottle

My emotions . . . my feelings . . .
are always of my own choosing . . .
my responsibility.
When sometimes
I make an unwanted choice . . .
choosing unhappiness . . .
anger . . . pain . . .
instead of the joy I want,
it is only from within me,
can I make a change.
Change never comes from within a bottle.
Its fumes may temporarily obscure
the truth about my pain.
It was my choice . . .
The bottle?
It is a cowards
way around that truth.

Shit Happens

The world is not for . . .
nor against me.
Shit just happens.
I choose my feelings . . .
my attitude . . . my viewpoint . . .
What may seem to be a misery . . .
could as easily be an opportunity.
And is always a lesson
from my soul.

Nah . . . Nah . . . Nah-Nah . . . Nah
Chapter 22

Destiny

One lone steel pin holding my life . . .
By all the laws, should have sheared . . .
cut through like butter . . . and didn't.
When I should have died . . .
expected to die . . . didn't.
Why?
I have a destiny . . . a life's purpose!
I know it now!

Knowing it is not complete,
has often troubled my sleep.
These many years I have lived . . .
asleep . . . in bed . . . in life.
Seeking the most comfortable rest.
Yet still experiencing . . .
in the cocoon of unconsciousness.
Learning . . . growing . . . awakening.

I grew from those experiences . . .
knew great love in the giving . . .
great sorrow in its ending.
Fatherhood . . .
being the model for a new life.
Doing my best . . .

just as did my father before . . .
and also falling short.

Short of the wisdom, the understanding . . .
Death's door opened up for me . . .
awakened my sleeping mind.
A mind destined to give this knowledge . . .
Impart it to my son . . .
that his son may grow up,
be shown better than once was he,
by me.
And become more, than ever I allowed,
me to be.

Shit Rubs Off

Being in the space . . .
the proximity, of the negativity . . .
affects.
A being of energy . . .
though with human body,
I still feel . . . still follow the flow . . .
and am drawn.
It is up to me, to keep me free . . .
away from . . . unaffected by . . .
negativity.
Because in the end,
shit rubs off . . .
and I too . . .
will stink.

Mr. Policeman, Sir

You are not my master . . .
You are not my God . . .
a superior being.
You are my esteemed servant,
there to protect me . . . save me . . .
from those who would abuse me,
not to be the abuser.
You are there to warn me of danger . . .
not threaten me with it.
There to aid me in emergency . . .
holding my life in your hands,
not squeezing my life, by your hands.
In you, I have placed my trust . . .
Are you trustworthy?
Can I trust you?
You . . . who deem yourself
better than me?

"F" Troop
Chapter 23

Not About Right Or Wrong

Life is not about right . . .
not about wrong . . .
the fairness to myself . . .
or others.
Life is about lessons.
A striving . . . a yearning . . .
to know the peace . . .
the joy of my soul.
It is not my right . . .
nor an expectation of my life . . .
to save others from their learning.
Yet, it is a joy,
and my right . . .
to offer my love,
and my light . . .
to uplift . . . empower . . .
those who are yearning.
To share my life's lessons
with those who are learning.

Quarrelsome People

Obnoxious people . . .
quarrelsome people . . .
are merely people of drama.
People with a need to be heard . . .
to be noticed . . .
to know that they matter.
They don't see how their need can be met
through friendship . . .
through love.
Perhaps as a child,
when expressing their love,
their loved ones did not know . . .
could not show . . .
its return.
So now . . . as then . . .
they cry out for love . . .
through drama
with attitude.
How I believe others regard me . . .
is how I regard me.
It is my attitude . . . my beliefs . . .
about me.
Attitude . . . my choice . . .

to be unhappy . . .
down . . . negative . . .
Blaming others, or life,
for my feelings.
Or choosing to revel in my life . . .
seeing the good . . .
feeling the joy . . .
loving myself.
Choosing responsible happy beliefs . . .
on how I regard me.

Sgt. Ego... Sgt. Compassion

Three skinny, starving . . .
begrimed, bedraggled men.
Begging for food.
Sergeant Ego . . .
looked through the eyes of judgment.
Saw only filth . . . loathsome insignificance.
Felt only his superiority . . .
his disdain . . . his hatred.
Sought only to acknowledge his ego . . .
to abuse . . . debase . . .
withhold their needs for life.
Keeping from them the abundance . . .
for which he cared naught.
Sergeant Compassion looked
through the eyes of love.
Saw only three fellow men,
three magnificent spirits . . .
in misfortune . . . in need . . .
asking his help . . .
for what they had not.
Felt only his love . . . his sense of truth . . .
the guidance of his heart.

Sought first to be of service . . .
sustain them in their need . . .
and then to understand.

My Soul For a Dream
Chapter 24

Double Standard

A married woman . . .
cheating on her husband
having relations with another.
From within, I feel my rage . . .
my condemnation of her seething.
Yet for the cheating man?
For him I feel a connection . . .
I understand his wants . . .
needs . . . passions.

Yet for her, of this,
I cannot see.
Does she not deserve her feelings too?
And yet, beneath it all . . .
their lives . . . their passions
are not of my concern.
They are not my business . . .
not for me to judge.
My feelings are from within . . .
chosen of my own wants . . .
my needs . . . my passions.
Do I want . . . expect . . . require,
my woman to be above it all?

To not have the same wants . . .
the same needs . . . passions?
The same as are within me?

Who She Was

The blinding light....
flash bulb of fresh love....
seeing only the shining beauty....
the acceptability of each other.
Being oblivious to any faults,
the possibility of any human weakness.
Soon gives way to other realities.
One farts . . . and belches . . .
even snores.
The other doesn't trust . . .
nor hold herself capable . . .
is insecure without control.
All things, which in the end,
must be accepted
or dealt with . . . in love.
I caved on my word . . .
gave her my power . . .
the control over me.
I wanted her love . . .
her company . . .
and paid the price.
For twenty-five years,

I paid the price.
Gave over control of my life . . .
gave up the respect I held for me.
I refused to see . . . to understand . . .
until Death came knocking
and woke me from the dream.
The dream of who . . .
she was to me.

Back In the World
Chapter 25

The Dragon of Fear

Apart . . . being apart . . .
through no choice . . .
leads to a longing
to be as one, once more.
And for me, a fear . . .
Would I never know this love again?
Am I not enough?
Enough to hold this woman's love,
strong enough for its return?
When once again,
I would claim
and be worthy of our oneness.
Yet the fear was only a little lizard
That sneaked into my mind . . .
And grew to be a dragon
named "Not Good Enough."

Surrogate Body

My pain of loss . . . and fear.
Fear of never seeing you again.
Fear created in my own mind . . .
led me to seek comfort of another's arms.
A sudden absence of you in my life . . .
The possibilities of a future without you . . .
my weakness . . .
the negative imaginings of my mind,
drove me to her . . . into her . . .
her surrogate body.
In truth . . .
I wanted only you

Help Me...

Help me Mom.
Help me Dad.
For I lack the strength to do this alone.
Oh, I know your buttons,
the ones to push . . .
the ones to get your help.
There is the one marked "pride."
The one marked "responsibility" . . .
marked "duty" . . . marked "right thing."
The "pride" of a parent,
in their "responsible" son,
for doing his "duty" . . .
doing the "right thing."
Yet, how my heart longs,
to again push the others.
The one marked "support". . .
the one marked "empower". . .
the one marked "heart's desire". . .
marked "love". . ."acceptance".
I want your "support," to "empower" my efforts,
in getting my "heart's desire".
Simply because you "love". . .
simply because you "accept". . .
me.

Great Pain—Great Lesson

Mom . . . Dad . . .
I made a choice in my life.
To be free from a prison . . .
a beautiful prison.
A wife who would never be . . .
never want to be . . .
the one I wanted . . .
who I needed.
Her choice . . . my choice.
The cost to my life . . .
great sorrow . . . agonizing pain.
Yet you saw only the wrong . . .
Your perceived wrong . . . your outrage . . .
You did not see my pain,
nor offer your love, your support . . .
your comfort.
You put the conditions . . .
of your perceptions . . .
rejections of my actions
upon your love.
I did not do what you wanted
and you withdrew your love . . .
your conditional love.
Why would you choose to feel in hate,
instead of in love....
with me?

Mom . . . Dad . . . A sincere "thank you"
for this lesson taught.
Those loved in my life,
will not be judged . . . nor rejected.
Not by me.
They will do what they do.
In that I may not always agree.
Yet, in their pain, in their need . . .
their grief . . .
at their side is where I'll be.
To uplift . . . support . . .
if ever they seek my help.
A tonic to their soul.
I choose to love them for who they are . . .
not just, for what they do.
That includes you . . .
too.

Victims, Drama, and Control
Chapter 26

The Blur of Love

You walk with weariness
out the door marked "Customs"
shoulders sagging
with the burden of your bags,
and a small frown knits your brow.
Then your face lights
as you spot me in the crowd.
And suddenly you are in my arms.
Hugging me . . . shaking . . .
tears streaking your make-up.
I am unable to speak
through the ache in my throat . . .
nor see,
through the blur of my love.

Faulty Programs

The beatings by Bart.
Then tied down . . .
gagged on stinking gritty socks
by the uncaring caretakers of an orphanage.
And later, lessons taught on icy steps,
in rejected fragile vulnerability.
Then forged into adulthood,
by the hammers of cruel abuse . . .
wielded in the best of military tradition.
All faulty programs of control . . .
Programs in the computer of my mind.
All saying . . . teaching . . . a law of falsity
that others, more powerful, control my life.
Others to be fearfully obeyed,
silently through the anger . . .
the burning acid of resentment.
Never understanding
it was always my choice . . .
to give away or to hold my power.
To be led by others . . .
or to walk on my own.
My own path . . .
the path of my own destiny.

Wand of Power

I know the anger.
Oh so well, I know it.
For too many years I owned it.
Stuffed inside . . .
only let out to spoil your day
whenever you were too happy.
And make you pay for my misery.

It was an anger of myself.
For not having the courage . . .
For not being man enough . . .
To let you go.
A self loathing I felt,
every time I whimpered . . .
every time I begged . . .
and pleaded with you to stay . . .
not to divorce me.

Looking back I see,
that it was only my own insecurity
programmed in from early childhood.
By being the ball

in a ping-pong game of life.
Pinged and ponged
one adult to another.
That led me to believe,
I was not good enough.

And I see it was the same for you.
The same game . . . the same programs.
Was it this attraction
drawing us together?
A sharing of insecurities?
I filled your need . . .
gave you your warranty . . .
It was never the divorce you wanted,
only the validation of my groveling.

I changed myself.
Found courage . . . self-respect.
Invalidated your warranty.
When you say "divorce"
I simply say, "okay."

And yet you stay.
And you know the anger.
You stuff it inside.
Whenever I am too happy,
you let it out.
Asking me to pay for your misery.

I cannot change you,
or provide you the security
as once I did.
Isn't it ironic . . .
your wand of power,
the thing I feared most . . .
lays limply in your hand.
A limp dick for you to use,
when pissing into the wind.

Marriage Vows of a Spiritual Warrior

With the dawning of this new day,
I, _____,
begin a new life together with
you, _____.
(Repeated in kind by the other)

Know in your heart,
that these promises I make
you will always know as truths . . .
truths spoken my soul to yours.
(Repeated in kind . . .)

I will strive above all
to stay in perfect love . . .
perfect integrity.
The joys of my heart . . .
the words of my lips . . .
and the actions of my hands . . .
will always align
perfect truth from me to you.
(Repeated . . .)

I will tell you my needs
and be conscious of yours . . .
Help you fulfilling them
in the space of love.
I will give you my love . . .
not the way I would want it . . .
rather in the way you
tell me you need it.
(Repeated . . .)

I'll always own my feelings . . .
never blaming them on you,
look for the shift . . .
the change indicated . . .
For whatever they are saying,
about me.
(Repeated . . .)

You are my partner in growth
on this journey called life.
I'll take your coaching of love . . .
for what I don't see about me
I will give you mine,
for what you are blind to, in you.
(Repeated . . .)

I'll never judge you as wrong,
for the things that you do . . .
nor for the way your
mind might believe.
What is "right" for me
is simply so for me . . .
it need. not be so, for you.
(Repeated . . .)

Know this in your heart:
it is with joy in mine
that I join my life . . .
my soul with yours.
I will travel with you
on this journey of life,
as long as we both want it so.
(Repeated . . .)

And if ever I feel
we are growing apart . . .
that the joy of my heart departs . . .
I will not lie you,
but speak what is truth,
without expectations from you . . .
And hear your response
to the depths of my heart.

(Repeated . . .)
>In the eternity of time
>should we part,
>your heart from mine,
>our parting will be as our starting . . .
>in honesty and truth and love.

(Repeated . . .)
(Then repeated together . . .)
>In honesty and truth and love . . .
>You are free to be YOU, with ME.

A Goosed Gander
Chapter 27

Saving

Saving . . . doing for others
that which they are capable
of doing for themselves,
is never appreciated.
In truth, What I am saying is,
"You are not competent . . ."
That I am "more able . . ."
"better than you."
And deep inside, you know . . .
you hear . . .
and are not grateful.

Hardships

My hardships, my difficulties, my problems,
are MINE, the creations of my mind.
It is my resistance to the situation
wherein lies my discomfort . . .
my unhappiness.
Far better to flow with . . .
float on the river of life,
than to fight the current.
Far better to search out the good . . .
the gain . . . in any situation . . .
than to resent or resist it.
The situation is in my life.
The discomfort . . .
is only in my mind.
I need to drop the rock,
the rock of my resentment,
or with a certainty,
it will drown me.

No Coincident

Coincidence . . .
A universal term for those un-believing
that there is a purpose . . . an order . . .
to the jigsaw puzzle of life.
That the cosmic power of the Universe . . .
the source . . . God,
has a plan . . . a purpose for us all.
It is what we have agreed to learn
in the creations of our lives.
That in putting forth our intention . . .
to gain the needs of our growth . . .
will always bring forth the means . . .
those "coincidences."
In finding one's destiny,
one's purpose . . . one's learning . . .
to surrender to it . . . to live it
is to live from one's heart
and to know the joy, the exaltation . . .
the magnificence of it all.
I have found my purpose in life,
my part in the universal puzzle . . .
and in the living,
am filled with awesome wonder.
No, there are no coincidences.

The Three Levels of Mind

My consciousness . . .
giving the orders . . .
determining my wants, my needs . . .
who I am.
My subconscious . . .
the provider, the servant . . .
taking the orders
of my conscious mind.
My Super conscious . . . my higher self . . .
the ultimate splendor that is my soul.
The gateway to, in touch with all . . .
a part of, and one,
with the Universe . . . with God.
My conscious mind operates . . .
controls the computer of my subconscious.
Writes the programs running me.
My subconscious creates . . .
manifests all my wants and needs . . .
using the power of the Universe,
made available by my Super consciousness.
Just as my creator created me,
I create my own reality.
And I have the power,
to create anything I want . . .
in it.

The Real Damage

We understood . . .
forgave one another.
Yet, the real damage
was within.
Much easier
me forgiving you . . .
than me, to forgive me.

When I'm out of integrity, I know.
I may dismiss it . . .
try to trick my conscious mind.
Yet, I can never fool my heart . . .
my higher self.
What it learns from me,
is that I am not to be trusted . . .
by me.

Integrity . . .
The congruence of thoughts,
words, and deeds.
My integrity . . .
is of the most importance,
to me.
Not yours.

Your lack of integrity
does no harm to me.
It only warns . . .
sets my level of belief
in you.
A lack of integrity in me,
does great harm to me.

It determines my level of belief
from you,
and more importantly . . .
from me.
It is my measure . . .
for self esteem.

Expectations

Jealous thoughts . . .
suspected betrayals . . .
have no place in my life.
My mind does not think about . . .
nor dwell upon such things.
For I have seen a glimmer . . .
have a dim understanding . . .
of the power of myself.
The great expectations of my life,
be it my most desired achievement,
or my greatest fear,
my higher self has the power
and will manifest it for me.
I have only but to dwell
my consciousness upon it
with emotion . . .
And it shall be mine!

Her Gift to Me
Chapter 28

Of Attitude And Responsibility

Attitude . . . one's viewpoint . . .
one's feelings about life,
make all the difference.
Determines . . . separates . . .
those desirable employees . . .
friends and lovers . . .
from those not.
It determines
those who are acceptable.

Having a good attitude
is to enjoy life.
The payoff of a bad attitude
is to avoid responsibility . . .
being able to blame others . . .
or circumstances . . .
for one's own unhappiness
or failures.

And no one wants to take the blame . . .
the responsibility
for another's negative feelings
or another's failures.
It was not a choice they made.
Why is this living in responsibility
so hard to accept?
It opens the doorway to happiness . . .
to a life of living . . .
to a life worth living.

Responsibility

Response-ability . . .
The ability to respond.
What is the manner of my responsibility?
For "response" clearly means a choice.
A choice?
No, MY choice . . .
on how I will act . . .
in how I will respond . . .
to the situation presented.
Will it be in a way that has meaning . . .
a benefit meant only for me . . .
though perhaps not one for you?
But . . . what if I found
a benefit for both . . .
a response giving to me . . .
And also, giving to you?
Would this not show . . .
would it not be . . .
an even greater responsibility?

Too Late

At first we were two . . .
me and you . . .
linked tightly together . . .
in love.
Then came Shane . . . in between.
To me, only the result . . .
the price of our love-making . . .
the price of my enjoyment of you.
Yet to you . . .
he was something you nurtured . . .
grew . . . supported awkwardly . . .
unselfishly for nine months.
Paid for with nauseous mornings . . .
with aching back . . .
with your forever full bladder . . .
and with a birth night's eternal hours
of mind straining . . .
body bending, blinding agony.
He was your creation . . .
your gift to the world.
He was your gift to me.
Something you wanted . . .

loved and appreciated . . .
more than ever I could know.
And although you offered,
held it all out to me . . .
I would not share in it with you.
Now acknowledged . . .
but late . . . so very late.
Yet while we both still live . . .
my son and me . . .
IS it ever too late?
Perhaps so . . .
But only for you and me.
Created by us both,
he is more than me.
For he still . . .
loves me.

Love Never Hurts

Lessons from my childhood . . .
from my youth . . .
That I am "not good enough,"
acceptable only on condition.
I was the receptacle,
the trash can for the anger . . .
the frustrations of an unhappy mother.
That the energy of my love . . .
my very dignity . . .
were hers to be taken,
whenever she wanted.
That my unwanted . . .
my very presence . . .
The child she couldn't have
always brought her pain.
I held myself apart,
distant from my son,
unwilling to bequeath to him
this nightmare . . . this legacy.
These same lessons.
But did I still?
Did I teach my son,

through his own experience of me,
that . . . love hurts?
Will he teach his sons the same?
Or will he do it better . . .
be a better man than me?
Teach his son that love uplifts . . .
heals . . . comforts.
Love never hurts!

Son

You are me . . . my genes . . .
my legacy . . . my gift to the world.
And yet . . .
will you also carry on my weakness,
as I did for my father?
Will you be unable . . . unwilling . . .
to share your love?
Will you withhold yourself,
your touch . . . your caress . . .
the loving words from your heart?
Or will you accept your son . . .
your own legacy?
Hold him close to your breast
and tenderly . . . honestly . . .
tell him of your love?
Teach him . . . enable him . . .
to accept himself, to love himself . . .
recognize in himself, the greatness . . .
the magnificence that is in you
and in me.
A magnificence I have never shown you,
because back then . . .
I did not see it in me.

Life Ain't Always Easy

Fair? Life ain't always fair.
Life just happens.
Fair is just a title . . .
a term I like to use.
And always . . .
is taken from the perspective
of my own mind.
A viewpoint others may not share.
Perhaps peace of mind requires
we all let go of "fair."
Accept what is . . .
find in it the good . . .
the benefit to it
for each.

The Freedom of the Country
Chapter 29

Life

Life . . . that to which
the human race clings so tenaciously.
Ravages indomitably survived . . .
famine . . . pestilence . . .
even the ultimate insanity—war.
All endured by the human spirit.
Clinging to life . . .
Mankind.

And yet . . . life . . .
at times, such a fragile thing.
Gone in an instant . . .
crushed . . . snuffed . . .
with the impact of screaming metal.
One instant, safe within the car's space . . .
the next, a mangled ruin of flesh
amidst a cloud of twisted steel, glass, and blood.

Or sometimes more insidiously taken . . .
slowly in self-loathing.
Misery in life . . .
unconsciously calls for death.

A minor injury and a blood clot,
formed by a subconscious
filled with negativity . . .
overflowing with self-hate.

Then broken loose,
it stops the lungs . . .
smothers the life.
The subconscious . . .
obeying
the self abusing call . . .
orders from an unhappy
conscious mind.

Today

Today is the only day there is.
Yesterday is gone . . .
dissolved to memories . . .
misty-eyed memories.
Tomorrow is as yet a dream . . .
a dream that may never come.
This life is only transitory . . .
a fleeting moment in time.
I may be gone . . .
dissolved into misty-eyed memories
in someone else's mind . . .
tomorrow.
Tomorrow is about changes . . .
changes I create in my life
right here . . . right now . . . today.
Today is the beginning . . .
or ending of my life . . .
today.

Sparring With The Dinosaur

Twelve years I rode the 350XL
Honda's trusty little Enduro.
Made for on or off the road.
I preferred the off . . .
dirt mountain roads . . .
sand swept trails . . .
the back country.
Colorado's mountains . . .
Utah's Canyonlands . . .
I loved it so.
Yet the highway . . .
the blacktop held a fear for me,
In competition with the gleaming hulks . . .
like sparring with the dinosaur.
I felt fragile . . . puny . . .
no match for them.
My fear was of being smashed . . .
just another bug smear,
spread across a bumper.
I parted with my XL . . .
old friend . . .
trusted companion . . .
moved to the city.

To Las Vegas . . . Sin City.
A blacktop jungle
full of crazies, drunks, and druggies.
A deadly . . . asphalt . . . battlefield.
Five years I cowered to the fear;
longing ever for the wind . . .
magic wind against my face.
Flying free beneath the slick rock cliffs
and mountains I loved so.
And for the power . . .
throbbing . . . rumbling . . .
surging between my thighs.
Then came the day I thought my last;
when I lay struggling for breath . . .
knowing . . . dreading the end.
Mourning all the wasted hours . . .
hours spent in fear . . .
hours spent not living.
That day, I thought my last,
was truly . . .
my wake up call to glory.
The glory I see within my soul . . .
A glory only I need to know.

These days, again I ride . . .
a machine more suited for the jungle.
A machine of ball busting, gut wrenching,
rumblin fury . . . my Virago 1100.
Now arriving home, I set the stand . . .
fresh off that asphalt battlefield.
I feel the tingle of adrenalin,
coursing sprightly with my blood . . .
and know . . . I am . . . alive!
I have sparred once more,
with the dinosaur . . .
and won.
And I know it is, just one more day,
that I have lived in truth . . .
a truth learned spoken
on the breath of death.
If I spend my life giving way to fear,
not doing because of the danger . . .
then I . . . am not . . . alive.
This life is full of danger.
It need not be full of fear.
Far better to recognize danger . . .
respect it . . . be aware . . .
even occasionally give it berth.

Yet never . . . give way to fear.
And in the end,
when death does come,
I will know . . . that I have lived!

Lessons of the Heart
Chapter 30

Navajo Mary Begay

Found frozen in the snow . . .
behind the state run liquor store.
Hair matted and fouled . . .
face stuck to the ground . . .
frozen tight, in a puddle of vomit.
No longer the sunny, bright eyed child
hair streaming . . . dancing to the drum . . .
flirting with the men.

Body bloated from a listless life . . .
of food stamps . . .
welfare money . . .
and alcohol.
Fouled with the release
of her bowel in death . . .
of the welfare system . . .
in life.

No longer the willowy sensuous woman . . .
smelling of flowers . . .
on her wedding night.
Married to her true love Benny Begay . . .
her long dead Benny . . .
lost to the battle fields . . .
of Vietnam.

Mary Begay . . .
now just a lifeless frozen heap
of tattered rags and unlived dreams . . .
A victim to the system . . .
to the booze . . .
to her grief . . .
to life.
And now in death . . .
purified in the arms . . .
of Benny.

Lake Powell

The sheer canyon walls
gleam ghostly in the moonlight.
Reflected palely in the glass smooth water
of the lake.
Troubled only by the slight ripples
sent out by our boat
as it rocks gently to our love.
Your eyes glow liquid in the darkness . . .
your body . . . eager beneath me.
The quickening harshness of our breath
and the slap of our bow
join the croak of a frog.
The only sounds to break the stillness
of the evening.
I am in love with the canyons
of Lake Powell.
And mostly . . .
I am in love . . .
with you.

Common Ground

How can love grow?
Where does it go
when there is no common ground?
When those things that please,
cause my heart to sing . . .
inspire . . . uplift . . .
my soul to flight,
hold nothing at all for you?
When instead of being
my breath of air . . .
an uplifting wind beneath . . .
you would rather be
the tether of my soul?
A rope of restraint,
my love for you . . .
holding me . . .
keeping me bound.
So magnificent, it could have been
two eagles flying . . .
wingtip to wingtip.
With similar dreams . . .
on a parallel course . . .

the same landmark
on the horizon.
And yet still . . .
the freedom of the skies.
Oh so high,
we could have soared,
our souls weightless . . .
with our love.

The Crack In The Wall

In life, we always give our all
to those we truly love.
Our all, according to our love . . .
our ability to give . . .
determined by the width of the crack,
the opening in the wall . . .
the walls around our hearts.
For it is from our hearts
that all love comes.
Tear down the wall . . .
allow love to flow
from an abundant courageous heart.
Does the wall protect
from what is without . . .
or imprison what is within?
It keeps us from loving . . .
keeps us from touching . . .
it keeps us apart,
from love.

Leaders... Traitors

Government officials...
leaders... traitors..
self-proclaimed Robin Hoods.
Taking from those who have...
giving it to those who don't.
But truth be told...
taking from those who work...
giving to those who won't.
Yet taking not quite enough
to raise the hackles,
the fight in the victim taken...
Only enough to get the support
the support of the victim given.
Yes, modern day heroes...
Congressmen... Senators...
buying the titles...
paying with the sweat
stolen off honest brows.
Buying support from those enslaved...
by having sold their souls.
Cheating them their chance...
their opportunity...

to know their own reliability . . .
in using their inner creativity . . .
and to experience the magnificence
of themselves.

Run Away

Leave all your problems . . .
your worries behind.
Run far away,
where they cannot find . . .
And yet . . . they always do.
Because they are never out there behind . . .
rather in here . . .
inside your mind.

Is This All There Is?
Chapter 31

Of Eagles And Barnyard Chickens

I lived my life for comfort . . .
always taking the easy way . . .
running from difficulties.
And yet . . .
the difficulties were only my perception,
as easily considered as challenges . . .
challenges to glory in . . . to conquer . . .
to grow by.
Instead, I lived life as a barnyard chicken.
Frantically flapping my wings
in near useless flight . . .
Squawking my indignation . . .
retreating . . .
running from the problems,
the adversities in my life.
Now I revel in them as challenges . . .
opportunities . . .
the warm air currents beneath
uplifting this eagle's wings . . .
raising my soul to heights . . .
unimaginable . . .
to the barnyard chicken.

Goodbye Jeffrey

Hello, it's me . . .
"Goodbye Jeffrey."
Saying "I'm leaving . . ."
saying "I'm gone . . ."
calling out to you . . .
"Draw me back . . ."
"Show me I'm wanted . . . needed."
"Tell me you love me . . ."
for I don't love myself.
I want your validation.
For I lack the courage . . .
the self respect . . .
to validate myself.
And I play this drama . . .
for control.
To get you to do it for me.
To make me feel worthy . . .
I ask you to do
what only I can do . . .
but won't.

Am I That Employee?

My work always shines
when I appreciate . . .
care about . . . value . . .
you.
When I give you my loyalty . . .
my esteem . . .
my hardest efforts.
Working for the money . . .
trading it for my time
only feeds my body.
Working with love . . ..
With someone I work with
for the joy it brings me,
Is what feeds my soul.

Perfect As God Made Them

The human body . . .
each one perfect as the creator chose.
Even in physical defect . . . perfect,
just as was intended.
A work of art to be appreciated . . .
covered only in protection of it's fragilities.
Why does Mankind cover it in shame?
Its exposure an embarrassment
to his sensibilities.
Does he not see . . .
it is only the thinking of his own mind . . .
not the naked human body,
that is filthy . . .
unwholesome in his own beliefs.
Therein lies the shame.
The hypocrisy . . .
blaming the sight of another's naked body
for the quickening of his own hormones . . .
the stiffening of his desire.
Yet both are perfect . . .
Perfect . . .
just as The Creator intended.

I, Macho Man

Macho Man . . .
hiding the pain . . . ignoring it . . .
pretending not to notice.
Putting on a show of strength . . .
of invulnerability.
Wearing the mask . . .
the pretense of someone stronger.
Covering the face . . .
my face . . .
of someone I thought weaker.
It is the face of someone
now strong enough
to admit the pain . . .
the honest concern . . .
that something may be wrong . . .
terribly, even fatally wrong.
Now, willing to recognize the danger
to listen to my body . . .
to feel the pain and to know:
Pain is my body's way of warning . . .
of calling out the danger.
"Hey, take notice of me . . .
I've something to say!
I want to say it . . .
while we both still breathe!"

Epilogue
The Ass-End of Assorted Poems

Body And Spirit

I look at our pictures,
the ones of you
and me together.
I see how dearly . . .
lovingly . . . I hold to you.

It is only now I see,
how in not one,
do you hold to me.
It was as pictured . . .
our life together.

Me loving you so deeply . . .
so completely . . .
seeing only . . .
feeling only . . .
my love for you

So many years . . .
living that wonderful,
that beautiful love story,
touching you . . . upholding you . . .
seducing your passion.

I never noticed . . .
took conscious thought,
of how in love's return
you cheated yourself
of loving me.

You could have had
the one you wanted,
yet settled for the man
you saw in me . . .
so dimly did you see.

As a wife, you excelled,
took care of your man . . .
That thoughtful care
I took for love . . . was love,
as you knew it to give.

You did your job well, a good wife . . .
though never my mate,
the woman of my soul.
I was not the one you accepted . . .
never the one you wanted.

Then came the day,
when Death reached for me,
clutching...choking...
smothering the life from my chest.
Then leaving me shaken...

Yet, with eyes wide open.
I saw...I knew, and would not die
knowing death but never a woman's love.
Loving me as I love her...
as I loved you and always will.

Blame

I left you . . .
You were not who I needed you to be.
My life's great aspirations . . .
its very purpose . . .
all . . . meant nothing to you.
You would not nurture
nor be a partner in my dreams.
And yet . . . that is not why.

That is just my ego
blaming you.
For blaming you is so much easier
than taking responsibility.
In truth . . . I wanted more
than you were willing to be.
The who I wanted you to be
was someone who uplifted me

Unwilling of accepting less . . .
I left.
If it is in my life,
it is ALL my responsibility.

MY life is not about you . . .
it is ALL about me.
And I cannot hold you responsible,
for anything . . . in MY life.

As For Me

I just want to be free . . .
to love and nurture me.
You are free to do . . .
free to be the same for you.
And somewhere in between . . .
if the two of us can meet . . .
Awesome!
Our love won't be a tie for binding . . .
rather, a rope for climbing.
As together we will journey . . .
together climb that mountain . . .
the mountain of our learning.

A Limp Dick No Longer

After twenty-five years we parted, Dear . . .
no longer willing to live in servitude,
begging you to stay . . . pleading for your love.
No longer accepting your control
nor my self disrespect.

You . . . not willing to change, to grow.
I needed you to see . . . for me.
But you were unwilling to look.
There might be a better way for us,
a better thought system.

One where joy is not in comfort,
rather in stretching . . . in growing . . .
Soaring like the eagle to unfamiliar heights,
Soaring on the uplifting currents of change
against the wings of our courage.

We parted, Dear . . .
Now both free to find the ones we want . . .
the ones who will nurture our souls.
For you, someone out there . . .
perhaps who wants a mother.

Someone comfortable . . . obedient . . .
Someone who won't stretch your life
with uncomfortable passions.
Someone to fill
that empty spot in your heart,
where once was I.

Someone safe enough . . .
yet strong enough . . .
to chase away the boogy man.
and perhaps . . .
Sergeant Conan.

And for me . . .
one who can nurture . . . be nurtured.
A courageous woman willing to grow . . .
wanting to soar . . .
to orgasm on the winds
of a turbulent . . .
passionate life!

And That Hero... Is Me

Throughout my life I lived always at effect.
Blaming others for my misfortunes...
for my grief.
Looking... forever looking... for my hero.

Someone to come...
to save me from myself...
to make my life work...
do it for me.

Until came the dawn, the awakening for me.
Death reached out...
shook me from my slumber...
to consciousness... to responsibility.

I drew forth my courage...
Faced...
what I feared most to see,
looked at what was inside of me.

Saw with delight, a magnificent surprise...
My hero was always right here, inside.
My hero was always... me.
Only I... can save me.

Back In The Graveyard of the Orphans

In the ghoulish green glare
of the monitor's stare,
I see him there . . .
once again.
Just as back then . . .
in the graveyard of the orphans.

Unstable lines chuckle in my mind
telling me more about me . . .
about what I now must see.
Leaves dancing with his breath
again, just as back then . . .
in the graveyard of the orphans.

The clench of his fist,
down deep in my breast,
he bestows his unseen gifts.
This time again, his touch is a friend,
just as back then . . .
in the graveyard of the orphans.

I feel him there,
on the antiseptic air . . .

It is the lies of my life
now killing me.
Placing me, in actuality . . .
in the graveyard of the orphans.

To live requires me to see
truth about my life and me.
For unlike back then,
innocence is as gone as my wind . . .
Only children run blind and win.
in the graveyard of the orphans

The life breath of my soul
must be courageous, you know.
For my journeys within . . .
now, just as back then,
is led by Death's ivory grin . . .
Led from back then . . .
from the graveyard of the orphans.

Follow Your Heart

Your heart is pure . . .
Your heart is kind.
Why play games . . .
with it in your mind?
Set it loose . . .
allow it to be free.
Let it show you . . .
what you will need,
to be who you . . .
want to be.

The Wonderment

Until you've looked inside yourself,
you'll never know the wonderment
of knowing just what you can do,
of seeing who you really are.
The depths of your courage . . .
the breadth of your heart . . .
the heights to which your soul can soar.
With so much magnificence to discover,
why . . . would you not want to find?
When only stopping you are your fears . . .
the imaginary dragons of your mind.

Changing You

I am awake with an ache in my heart.
Awakened by the merest glimmer of light,
illuminating my darkened mind.
It's not the all-seeing brightness
of God's light
revealing everything with understanding,
peace, and joy;
but merely a dim glimmer,
illuminating the darkness of my slumber
and bringing me to consciousness.

I am awake!
And my heart aches as I look upon you,
my beauty, my wife.
You sleep, still,
like most of humanity slumbering on.
Never suspecting the magnificence
and power you possess.
I take you tenderly in my arms,
and gently urge you to awaken.

Yet, you slumber on.
I shake you . . .
rattle your very bones!
And your dreams only become nightmares,
with me, an unrecognizable ogre.
Sadly, my consciousness has only
troubled your peaceful repose.
And my heart aches to show you
the wonder of yourself.

Oh Meg! I am awake . . .
And it is MY ache . . .
MY ache within MY heart.
I can find peace within myself.
And yet . . . I am your nightmare,
where I want only to be
your sweetest dream.
Only be to changed within you, by you.
It can never be . . . by me..

Mind Talk

I am who I think I am . . .
I become who I tell myself to be.
Even in jest, when I affirm a thing,
my higher mind believes.
For it has no sense of humor . . .
does not see the joke.
It simply trusts in me . . .
does not believe I would lie . . .
that I would do harm to me.
It only manifests my desires . . .
and beliefs.
I need always watch my mind talk,
believe in, and be kind,
to me.

Setting Up The Win

This book in the writing was a win for me.
Yet, for me, the ultimate win
is a life worth counting.
My life of meaning . . . of winning . . .
being also of meaning . . .
a win for you too—win/win.
And so it is, I set up this win . . .
I do not say,
it was my birthday yesterday . . .
Instead, I say,
it is my birthday, today.
Come, share this day with me.
Gift me with what my life . . .
for you . . .
now means.

About The Author

Edmond E. Frank a.k.a.
E. Egorhh Frank

When one has experienced and seen the end of one's life, there comes a bottom-line knowing that what is of most importance is to be honest with oneself. This is your life—you only get the one. Are you reaching for the true joys of your heart? Or are you giving yourself away, living your life to suit the wants of others, as society demands. Such knowledge is not taught in any institution. It is a rare and uniquely precious understanding that Ed has, and shares.

Adopted at the age of four, Ed lived a *normal* life for his first forty-five years. As a mechanic, he existed from paycheck to paycheck, just getting by, doing what was expected. It was only with the imminence of death that he finally realized how he was someone he didn't like or respect. Living one's life to please others always has that effect.

Now a Personal Life Coach and writer, he is living proof that we all, at any point in life, can change to become the "who" we really want to be.

Through his writing, he offers change to others. It does not necessarily take meeting the Angel of Death to catalyze change. Unlike with Ed, that angel seldom gives us the gift of a second chance. Ed's novels gives a layman's view of how change is done, its price, and of the magnificent adventure found in living the life of one's dreams.

Here are a few facts about Edmond E. Frank, also known to his friends as Egorhh—his middle name—or "Coach Egorhh" to some.

- ➢ Majored in Geology at the University of Utah.
- ➢ Vietnam era vet—Army honorably discharged.
- ➢ Lived some years abroad—Australia, Greece, and Korea.
- ➢ A creative artisan, silversmith, and lapidist.

- A committed father and ex-husband.
- A man who has worked through the pain of divorce, lost everything he once thought important in life, and started over again, living a life of real importance to his soul.
- Is a poet and author of ten books (currently).
- A man who has done his own healing work.
- He is a Personal Life Coach—Graduate of Coach University and the WeCoach training programs.
- He knows and lives Spiritual Law.
- He is a teacher, mentor, and a servant leader.
- He has volunteered countless hours in self-help seminars supporting others in their growth.
- A man who is familiar with experiential workshops, ropes courses/high wire events,
- Familiar with Reiki, NLP, HPP, Silva and many other forms of meditation.
- Has participated in Native American sweat lodges.
- As is a biker he rode with the American Legion Riders.
- We was the first State Captain for the Nevada Patriot Guard.
- The last twelve years of his working life he served the disabled as a Para Transit bus driver. Seeing first-hand what his clients had to deal with in their lives, was a truly humbling experience.

Coach Egorhh is a man of passion and compassion who knows how, and lives life fully. Bottom line: Ed is one of those, who has learned to love himself. This is the first requirement for having the ability to love others.

He currently resides in Las Vegas, Nevada, and no longer coaches one-on-one in person or over the phone. As a writer and published author, he finds he can reach out and touch many more minds through his books than he ever could as a practicing Personal Life Coach.

This current book is comprised of the poems removed from his first novel, *Soul of an Eagle*. Both novels were based on his memoirs. Published back to back with Book Four in his Redneck Spirituality series on spiritual laws (authored under the name E. Egorhh Frank) they may well be his last.

His Redneck Spirituality Series are workbooks meant to be worked. And it's okay if some folks just want to read it, up there, in the bleachers, above the field of life. Not everyone has the courage to play down here on the field—much less acknowledge it as "Rumi's Field." What about you?

Again, the novel these poems were originally used to illustrate, *The Courage of a Butterfly*, is based on his real life and tells the story fully and in depth, however he didn't write any of his books to tell his story—everyone has one. He wrote them to show you what *New Thought* is about. You can order all of his books through Barns and Noble or Amazon. Or, if you have a favorite bookstore they likely can get it for you as well.

NOTE:

Honesty in all my writing is important to me. It is industry standard to have someone else, real or pretended, write about the author in third person—no one likes a braggart. This section is written in the conventional third person format—but in honesty—by me, the author.

Works by This Author
Edmond E Frank

The Courage of a Butterfly
(a novel)

A Butterfly's Transformation—
In POETRY

* * *

The Soul of an Eagle
(the sequel)

An Eagle's Flight—
In POETRY

Works Authored As
E. Egorhh Frank
"Coach Egorhh"

Redneck Spirituality—Series
Book One
Book Two
Book Three
Book Four
Books One & Two Combined
(in print form only)

www.ingramcontent.com/pod-product-compliance
Lightning Source LLC
Chambersburg PA
CBHW020527080526
44583CB00013B/775